Coastal Waters
Images of North Carolina

photography by
Scott Taylor

Published by **Coastal Waters Publishing**

214 Pollock St, Beaufort, NC 28516
www.ScottTaylorPhoto.com

First Edition - Second Printing

Book design by Whitline Ink Incorporated
Printed in China by C&C Offset Printing Co.,Ltd.

Applied for Library of Congress Cataloging-in-Publication Data
ISBN 0-9767606-0-6

This book is dedicated to my late aunt, Ann Duncan Brown. Her generosity allowed me to experience the wonders of the North Carolina coast from an early age through my college years and beyond. Thanks Aunt Ann.

acknowledgements

Thanks to Andy Scott of Coastal Carolina Press for sharing his vision of Coastal North Carolina and publishing the first printing of this book, Bland Simpson for allowing me to experience the Cedar Island Wildlife Refuge in his trusty Jon boat, Lenore for keeping me focused, and my family and friends for their years of undying faith and support. A special thanks to my son David for asking me "Why does a guy from Cleveland want to spend time in a place like this?"

foreword

What a wonderful thing it is to behold and to *experience* the work of such a highly skilled lensman as Scott Taylor of Beaufort, North Carolina. Though yet a young man, Taylor is a mature artist indeed, fully committed to and intimately involved with his longtime subject, the Carolina coast.

Taylor is one of the premier visual interpreters of our coast's natural and human world. We have seen his work in *Coastwatch*, in *Wildlife in North Carolina*, in marine lab publications from Piver's Island, and in others from such groups as the North Carolina Coastal Federation and the North Carolina Coastal Land Trust. Just as we think of Winslow Homer and his ties to Prout's Neck in Maine, of Ansel Adams and Yosemite, so, similarly, many of us have come to think of Scott Taylor's photography as being inextricably identified with the creeks, rivers and sounds, the marshland byways and the wondrous barrier islands. In Taylor's down-home elegance and pictorial presentation, we may also sense a link to another Carolinian, the brilliant have-camera-will-travel artist from New Bern and, later, Chapel Hill, Bayard Wootten. Mrs. Wootten captured the powerful way coastal waters pile cumulous clouds high above them and then reflect that splendor, and now Taylor carries on the campaign in the ocean and sound country regions, reporting back in a panoramic style all his own.

As we gaze at the *Closed Area No Shrimping* sign marooned in the marshgrass of Rumley's Hammock in the Cedar Island National Wildlife Refuge, or at the stark message painted across the window-glass of a Live Oak Street seafood market in Beaufort, we cannot fail to apprehend Taylor's concern for the health of our coastal waters. In the picture of McIntosh's Seafood Market, the jollity of the jumping fish is belied by the owner's declaration in the window, his personal word on the disastrous, pandemic red tide that shut down shellfishing on the coast in late 1987, and here, too, is Taylor's salute to the documentary work of Walker Evans, Dorothea Lange, and Arthur Rothstein.

Much of Taylor's work in this collection is land-and-sky-water-scape. Yet just as many images marvel over what an enormous amount of *activity* is always going on in this part of the world. Men are spot fishing in the hook of Cape Lookout, with pelicans in flight nearby, and sunlight glancing off the big skiff and shimmering in the shallows, a grand fair-weather day at the edge of our province. A lone man in a sou'wester bails his small sailboat in Taylor's Creek during Hurricane Charley, as a Coast Guard boat glides along in the background, a grim gray sky low and looming. Sunlight streams through a pile of clouds off Bald Head. Carrot Island ponies gallop

through the shallows one April day. ("The only time of the year," says Taylor, "that they do anything but graze.") One night the fish factory in Beaufort is all ablaze with lights; one morning a big pogey boat appears in the ghostly fog. A Chowan River poundnetter faces astern with a boatful of fish before him — pleased? exhausted? or both? — as the boat moves toward the rivershore.

One stunning portrait Taylor presents to us is that of the mists on Taylor's Creek early on a winter's morning, one of those times that gave Bob Simpson the evocative title for his memorable book, *When the Water Smokes*. In Taylor's photograph, the water is smoking all right, and the boats almost seem to be entranced on a silver river.

And just look at how much an initially placid picture like the one of Piver's Island skiffs is really showing us. A trawler is moored in Taylor's Creek behind what was then Barbour's Marine, a parts-and-machine shop operation for the fishing trade that in the mid-1990s yielded its space to purveyors of pastries and coffee and chardonnay. Well beyond this in the picture's background, beneath a golden morning sky, a thin, dark stream of smoke — laden with the awesome pungence of menhaden cooking down into fishmeal — slides away from town by the grace of the north wind. In this volume's final image, water trails off the tail flukes of a young humpback whale just a split second before the great creature completes its dive — and one can almost hear the plunge.

The late Dirk Frankenberg, who knew and loved our coast with a great intelligence and passion, chose two of Taylor's photographs for the cover of his book *The Nature of North Carolina's Southern Coast* and employed more of them inside as well. No wonder — Scott Taylor has been there at the complex and many-chambered heart of the coast and borne witness to its rhythms and mysteries through all weathers and all seasons. His many splendid images, his close and masterful observations, are a powerful encouragement to all of us to regard our own moments hereabouts with ever more appreciation and to sharpen our vision of all the shore life around us, of the great sea beyond, and to enjoy and explore it all as much and as devotedly as he has.

This collection will quickly become a favorite in many a library, and no author could wish for more. Such is the artistry, and the well-deserved success, of Beaufort's Scott Taylor.

Bland Simpson
Chapel Hill, North Carolina
June 2000

introduction

It was late autumn, 1998, when my son, David, and I loaded Bland Simpson's well-traveled Jon boat with camera gear and headed north up the thoroughfare toward Rumley's Hammock in the heart of the Cedar Island Wildlife Refuge. Fall is my favorite time of year on the marsh — the grasses are just beginning to lose their green, the winds shift north clearing the summer haze and the sun moves lower in the sky, lengthening the late afternoon shadows.

We had been on the water about an hour when my son, then leaning over the precipice of his teenage years, asked me a question I'll never forget. "Dad, why does a guy from Cleveland, Ohio want to spend so much time in a place like this?" I knew that no matter what I said, it could be years before he might understand, if at all. But I also knew that he would come to appreciate these afternoons — perhaps much later.

As we approached the hammock I noticed that spectacular mare's tale clouds were forming in the sky over Core Sound. I scanned the horizon for the spot — the perfect foreground to complete my composition. A patch of marsh along the shore looked promising. Quickly anchoring the boat, I jumped out in knee-deep tannic water, grabbed my favorite camera and headed toward the marsh. Distant marsh grass began to glow. My pulse quickened. The image began to take shape. I envisioned the camera angle as I plodded into the marsh. One shot here, perhaps another angle over there, then kneeling into the pungent marsh for one last exposure, or maybe two. I headed for the boat, pausing to rinse the thick black marsh mud off my legs. The anticipation of that night's dark-room work was already building.

When I travel the coastal waters of North Carolina I see a world of images. I see changes — tidal and seasonal, natural and man-made, begging to be captured on film. I feel the salt on my face and my camera lens as I wade through the rich coastal waters. My desire is to offer this experience to others through my images. I want them to feel the salt on their sun-tightened cheeks, smell the rich aroma of the intertidal zone, and feel their pulse quicken at the sound of dolphins breaching near shore.

Bald Head Beach

Phalarope — Beaufort

Fort Macon Beach

Cast Net — Atlantic Beach

Gill Net—Cedar Island

Trawler *Anna Marie*

Blue Crabs

Early Morning off Cape Lookout

Wanchese

The Point — Cape Hatteras

The Hook — Cape Lookout

Mackerel Sky — Beaufort

Nasty Harbor — Beaufort

To the Beach — Shackleford

Shackleford Beach

High Dune   Shackleford Banks

Maritime Forest — Shackleford Banks

Cape Hatteras Point

Fresh Catch — Morehead City

White Oak River — Swansboro

Sand Fence—Atlantic Beach

Camille → Beaufort

Taylor's Creek — Beaufort

McIntosh Seafood Market — Red Tide

Coming Home — Taylor's Creek

Hurricane Charley — Beaufort

Nor'easter—Atlantic Beach

Skiff — Beaufort

Small Boat Dock — Duke Marine Lab, Beaufort

Tradewinds Tackle Shop — Ocracoke

Surf Fishing—Ocracoke

Heading Out — Taylor's Creek

Offshore Trawl

Town Creek — Beaufort

Mary Catherine

Foggy Morning on Taylor's Creek

Nasty Harbor Night

Smell of Money — Beaufort

Menhaden Boats — Beaufort

Cape Lookout Lighthouse

Cape Hatteras Lighthouse

Ocracoke Lighthouse

Cat — Beaufort

Herring Fishing on the Chowan River

Offshore — Beaufort Inlet

Atlantic Beach

Fort Macon Jetty

Swansboro

Basket of Blue Crabs

Lady—Highway 12

No Shrimping—Rumley's Hammock

Better Days—Off Highway 12, Cedar Island

Cedar Island Beach

Rumley's Hammock Beach

Rumley's Hammock

Core Sound 1

Marsh — Off Highway 12

Cedar Island Wildlife Refuge

Highway 12 — Lola

Cedar Island Wildlife Refuge

John Day's Ditch — Cedar Island

Pony Prints in the Sand

Carrot Island Pony

Shackleford Banks Ponies

Pony Roundup — Shackleford Banks

Henry Piggot House — Portsmouth

Styron–Bragg House — Portsmouth

Portsmouth Island

Church on Portsmouth Island

Graveyard — Portsmouth

Sea Captains' Graves — Portsmouth

Graveyard — Shackleford Banks

Ghost Forest — Shackleford Banks

Pelican at Rest

Egret in Flight

Ibis

Egret

Shackleford Banks Ponies

Shackleford Banks Ponies

Grazing Ponies — Shackleford Banks

Swail — Shackleford Banks

Carrot Island Ponies

Thundering Ponies — Town Marsh

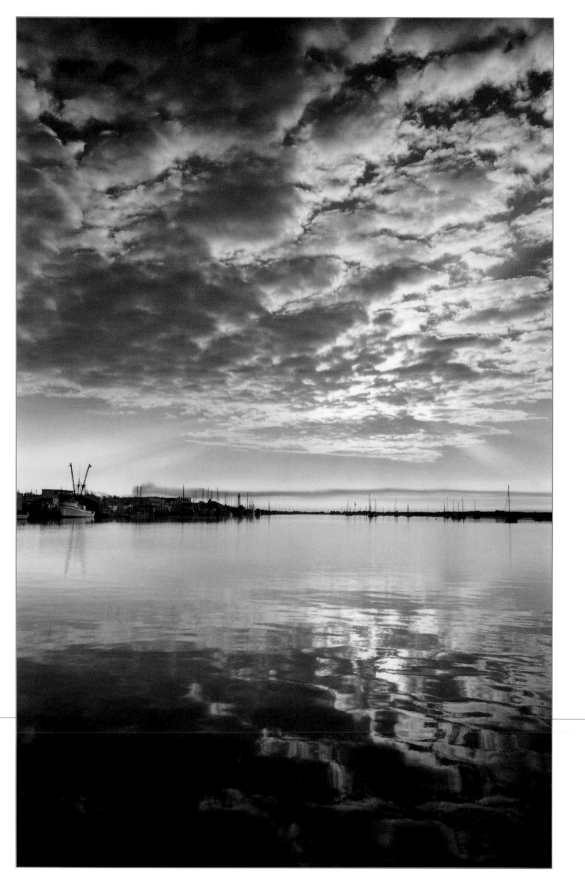

Beaufort

Dolphins — Beaufort

Whale off Cape Lookout